IMAGES
of America

SHELDON

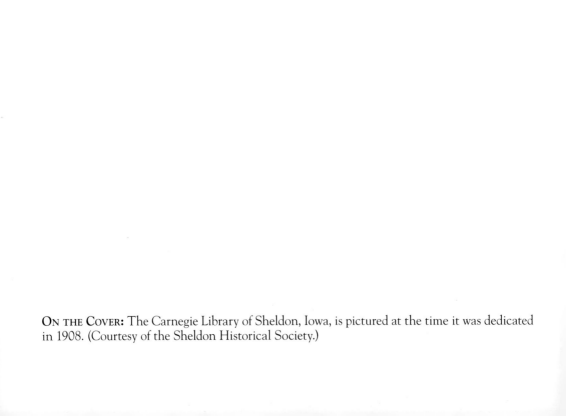

IMAGES
of America
SHELDON

Thomas J. Whorley

Millie Vos

Enjoy!

Thomas J. Whorley and Millie E. Vos

ARCADIA
PUBLISHING

Copyright © 2022 by Thomas J. Whorley and Millie E. Vos
ISBN 978-1-4671-0889-8

Published by Arcadia Publishing
Charleston, South Carolina

Printed in the United States of America

Library of Congress Control Number: 2022941619

For all general information, please contact Arcadia Publishing:
Telephone 843-853-2070
Fax 843-853-0044
E-mail sales@arcadiapublishing.com
For customer service and orders:
Toll-Free 1-888-313-2665

Visit us on the Internet at www.arcadiapublishing.com

This book is dedicated to Israel Sheldon, the man for whom Sheldon was named. He was a director of the Sioux City & St. Paul Railroad. Israel Sheldon foresaw the westward growth of the United States and would be proud of his city namesake—even though he never came to visit! (Courtesy of the Sheldon Historical Society.)

CONTENTS

ACKNOWLEDGMENTS

Images of America: *Sheldon* was started over a year ago by the two of us working nights and weekends gathering photographs, researching information, reading articles from old newspapers, and writing captions. We plowed through notebook after notebook, folder after folder, and file cabinet after file cabinet documenting dates in search of information and pictures. We also utilized the *Sheldon Area Centennial Book* as a resource for gathering information. We struggled with picture quality and limitation of words. Some pictures we wished we could have included did not meet publisher quality and standards for the book.

The task involved several dedicated individuals and organizations that we would like to thank. First of all, thanks to the Prairie Queen Museum and Sheldon Historical Society for granting us access to the museum and historical society archives. We would also like to thank Peter W. Wagner, publisher of the *Northwest Iowa Review*, for allowing us to search its photograph files for old pictures, some of which were utilized in the book. A special thanks goes to Myrna Wagner of Iowa Information Publishers and Printers for her dedicated work in organizing, scanning photographs, and guiding us in the layout of the book. Her work was invaluable, and without her assistance, the book would not have been possible.

A special thanks to Ashley Gordon for word processing, organizing titles in the manuscript, and proofreading. Also, thanks to Gillian Mohn for her early work in layout categories and page collation.

Our thanks to Jeff Reutsche, who got things started for us at Arcadia Publishing, and our editor, Caitrin Cunningham, for keeping us on task and meeting deadlines for publication. Thanks also to Ryan Vied for her assistance in editing.

We wish to thank our families for their patience and allowing us to take on this project.

If we have erred on dates or facts, they are ours alone and we apologize. The book covers a period from 1872 to the 1970s. We were limited on words and pictures, so perhaps someone may want to pick up from here and write a volume two.

We also want to thank the Ralph Hollander family for allowing us to reprint the introduction written by historian Ralph Hollander, "The Times of Israel Sheldon."

Samuel Johnson once said, "The greatest part of a writer's time is spent in reading, in order to write; a man will turn over half a library to make one book."

We welcome your comments on the book, and you can write to us at the Sheldon Historical Society, PO Box 35, Sheldon, Iowa, 51201 or email at Tom.Whorley828@gmail.com. We are happy to present these images of our hometown. We hope you enjoy the book as much as we have enjoyed putting it together.

All images are courtesy of the Sheldon Historical Society unless otherwise noted.

—Thomas J. Whorley and Millie E. Vos

INTRODUCTION

After the Civil War, thousands of Grant's and Sherman's more adventurous soldiers sought a new start in life on the opening frontiers west of the Mississippi. Here, the immense fertility of America's mid-continent grasslands now could be exploited because of the cheap transportation made possible by railroads.

In St. Paul, an ex-general named E.F. Drake saw opportunity in a north–south railroad to Sioux City and Omaha. While seeking capital for his adventure in New York, Drake met Israel Sheldon, a smart self-sufficient financier, who helped him get the Sioux City & St. Paul Railroad organized. One of the stations was named for Sheldon.

Returning to St. Paul, Drake engaged another ex-general named Justin Wade Bishop to oversee construction of the new railroad. Finding a route was easy. Mostly old Indian trails showed the best way through Minnesota. In Northwest Iowa, the trail followed the Floyd River valley, formed 10,000 years before when melting glacial waters searched out the most level route to the Missouri River. That little river had been named by Lewis and Clark in honor of Sgt. Charles Floyd, the only man lost on their expedition.

As Bishop's rails cut across the prairie that summer of 1872, scarring its pristine beauty forever, he noted that on July 4 they would arrive at the base of the mound selected for the town of Sheldon. His draftsman, H.C. Randall, had already drawn the plat. On July 4 and on the top of that mound, General Bishop arranged for a patriotic picnic for his men, a few dozen homesteaders, and businesspeople who awaited his arrival. It was a happy, hopeful occasion. Everybody felt they were making history on this desolate little hill with not even a tree in sight.

Their names rang of a Yankee heritage—Lane, Jones, Perkins, Piper, Bradley, Parkhorst, Frisbee, Logan, Robison, and others similar. Later, there would be an influx of German and Irish names of men who came to help build the nation's railroads and then stayed to homestead its free lands. The area today abounds with highly efficient, specialized industries developed from within, some with national and international customers. After 1900, hundreds of Dutch names would spill over from colonies in neighboring Sioux County where immigrants from Holland had settled to farm the rich soil.

With these of European stock added to its Yankee American core, Sheldon enjoyed a steady, prosperous growth characterized by Christian traditions, a strong thrift and work ethic, and a keen appreciation of the value of education.

Agribusiness remains the dominant industry, but those hearty industrious early-day pioneers who chose Northwest Iowa for their homes said this was "the garden spot of the world." I believe they were right.

One

TRAINS AND PLANES

The first railroad was called the Sioux City & St. Paul Railroad, later changed to Chicago, St. Paul, Minneapolis & Omaha Railroad. The Milwaukee Railroad arrived in Sheldon in 1878 and was known as the Iowa Dakota Railroad. Accurate records cannot be located on the arrival of the Illinois Central Railroad. The branch line extended from Cherokee, Iowa, to Sioux Falls, South Dakota. The Illinois Central Railroad was formerly called the Yazoo & Mississippi Railroad. The railroads were a significant part of Sheldon's history and were a great benefit to Sheldon's early development. It was very unusual for a town to have three railroads passing through on a daily basis.

In the summer of 1924, Sheldon suffered the worst train wreck in its history. The tragedy occurred when the engine of a southbound passenger train derailed north of Sheldon. Two people were killed, and many were injured. Residents utilized cars to help transport the injured to local hospitals. The hospitals were soon full, and the doctors were forced to accommodate patients on the porches.

The most unusual train wreck in Sheldon's history took place within the city limits in 1905 outside Union Depot. A special car belonging to the superintendent of railroads was hooked on the rear of a freight train that was stopped on the crossing of the train heading west. Another train was coming from the south and rammed the superintendent's car.

The most expensive train wreck is one that occurred south of Sheldon in 1960. Fifteen cars derailed as a result of a track washout. The derailed cars were loaded with prize hogs headed for the state fair.

In the early 1900s, there was a lunchroom operated by Nettie Thill across from the depot. Passengers used to wait their turn at the counter and tables. Sheldon had a train every 30 minutes year-round for a total of 18 passenger trains a day.

Sheldon air shows drew national recognition. Some of the greatest flying aces were up in the clouds performing unbelievable feats to thrill thousands. Crowds were estimated at nearly 10,000 at the air shows that took place for nine years, commencing in 1932. One of the features of the great air shows was the demonstration of acrobatic flight by John De Hoogh, a Navy aviator instructor and Sheldon farmer. All roads led to Sheldon for these spectacular air shows. Sheldon was known as Iowa's greatest air show. The first airport was located near Ritter in 1942. In June 1943, a tornado struck the airport hangar at Ritter and destroyed nine planes. The wind was estimated at 62 miles per hour.

Sheldon owes its existence to the mighty iron horse with steam belching from its smokestack. Railroads built hundreds of miles across barren prairies and were responsible for creating towns on their routes, which created businesses and houses in the newly developed towns. With a puff of smoke and the scream of a whistle, Sheldon was founded on July 3, 1872. This 4-4-0 locomotive was built in 1884. (Courtesy of Cornelius Koele.)

A Milwaukee locomotive with a coal car was a familiar site in Sheldon. The Milwaukee Railroad arrived in Sheldon in 1878 and stayed an active rail line until the Milwaukee Agency closed in 1980. Sheldon also had the Illinois Central Railroad and the Chicago, St. Paul, Minneapolis & Omaha Railroad passing through.

In August 1905, a railroad collision occurred between two steam locomotives by the railroad depot, called Sheldon Junction. The Union Depot south of Sheldon replaced Sheldon Junction when it was destroyed by fire.

The first depot was built in 1887 and was called Sheldon Junction. In 1906, it burned down, and a new depot was built in 1907 and called Union Depot. This was one of the first places that people gathered socially. The depot is now the home of the farmer's market each week during the summer.

Large crowds gathered at the depot waiting to greet Teddy Roosevelt on September 3, 1910. People turned out in their very best clothes. Roosevelt was campaigning as a presidential candidate for the Bull Moose party. Someone in the crowd threw him a teddy bear, and the crowd joined in unison, "Long live Teddy!"

Teddy Roosevelt, former president of the United States, stopped in Sheldon and gave a short speech on the back of the train in 1910. His speech emphasized "a square deal all around."

The American Bicentennial Freedom Train, with a red, white, and blue "Spirit of 1776" engine No. 4449 pulling 28 cars, stopped in Sheldon on Saturday, September 6, 1975. Hundreds gathered along the tracks. The stop was to take on water and switch tracks before moving on to Sioux Falls, South Dakota. The 23,000-gallon tanks needed 10,000 gallons of water.

The last serious train wreck occurred in 1953, when one winter afternoon a snowplow collided with the Chicago, St. Paul, Minneapolis & Omaha passenger train No. 203. The 203 was going south, and the snowplow was headed north. The two hit head on. The engineer of the passenger train was killed, and many people were injured.

This modern hangar at the Sheldon Municipal Airport could hold 10 planes. The new hangar was located near Ritter, Iowa.

This airplane on the bed behind a truck appeared at a special parade held in Sheldon promoting flying. The airport at Sheldon was only one of six flying schools that were approved by the federal government as a civil air training center in 1943. At one time, there were more licensed flyers in Sheldon based on population than anywhere in the United States. In 1942, Sheldon held Chapter No. 1 of the National Aeronautic Association.

Sheldon's first air show in 1932 was held in a pasture. Sheldon had a reputation for being air-minded and hosted the largest air show in Iowa. With the help of federal Work Progress Administration (WPA) funds, the pastures were converted to an airport. The last air show in Sheldon was held in 1941.

Col. Roscoe Turner, a racing pilot at the height of his flying career, made a personal appearance at the Sheldon Municipal Airport in 1938, and the airport honored him by naming the Sheldon airport Roscoe Turner Airport. Turner had won several international air races, had appeared in films, and was often photographed either with a movie star or an African lion that flew with him in his two-seater plane.

A 62-mile-per-hour wind in June 1943 tore the roof off a hangar and destroyed nine planes beyond repair. The administration building had its doors torn off with serious damage to the roof. The wind lasted for 30 minutes, with over two inches of rain, and the surrounding buildings received extensive damage.

Alta Mae Gintert Ruby (left) signed up for the Civil Air Patrol in January 1944 to show patriotism for her country. She took classes with a squadron of 85 members in a Sheldon airport classroom, and after 10 hours of flight training with an instructor, she flew her solo flight.

Two

BUSINESSES AND FIRES

Sheldon businesses have been a center of robust retail sales. Sheldon is ideally situated at the junction point of four counties. In all that is good in Iowa, the finest is in Northwest Iowa. It is the center of some of the world's finest farmland.

The main shopping area in Sheldon is conveniently located along the main streets. With the expansion of the Highway 60 expressway on the eastern portion of the city, the outlying areas have also grown businesses. A variety of stores offer a large selection of merchandise with convenient municipal parking. Retail promotions are scheduled throughout the entire year by an active retail committee of the Sheldon Chamber and Development Corporation. Friendly clerks and clean, modern, well-kept retail stores greet the avid shopper. Sheldon offers a variety of professional services, financial services, law enforcement, fire and ambulance services, reliable utilities, adequate transportation systems, and efficient government by a city manager, mayor, and city council.

Sheldon offers great amenities, including many restaurants, a recreational trail, a stunning new event center, indoor and outdoor swimming pools, new soccer and baseball fields, indoor racquetball and wallyball courts, outdoor tennis and pickleball courts, a running track, weight training, exercise classes, a skate park, and various parks.

Sheldon has experienced 13 major fires since 1885. The worst was in 1888, when fire took out almost all of Third Avenue. As a result, all downtown construction was required to be brick only. The fire department used water from cisterns to fight the 1888 fire, but in 1894, a water tower was built to supply water for fires.

Another memorable fire was in 1958, when a large portion of west Third Avenue was destroyed. Ellerbroek's, Starrett's, and the Arlington Annex were totally destroyed, while Strak's and Faust Rexall Drug had water and smoke damage.

In 1879, John and Harry Iselin built the first flour mill and 18 cottages that employees could rent. This part of Sheldon was called Iselinville. In that first year, the mill had 35 employees and ground 650,000 bushels of grain. Due to financial difficulty, the mill was closed after less than two years of operation. Later, Scott Logan purchased, remodeled, and reopened the mill.

Clouds of steam from the Iselin Mill marked the Sheldon skyline as the burrstones ground flour and meal.

The official Sheldon Centennial Symbol was adopted in 1972. It was a distinctive modern picture of a young lady with auburn hair drawn and colored by Hal Tuttle, a former Sheldon art teacher, which represented the name of the premium grade of flour milled by Prairie Queen Mill and the original Sheldon nickname, "Queen City of the Prairie." The young lady originally appeared on a cornmeal product from the Prairie Queen Mill.

Pictured is the Scott Logan Flour Mill. The Big Four Mill is in the distance on the right. Logan's other mill is the white building next to the flour mill. The Illinois Central depot is in the distance.

PRAIRIE QUEEN MILL
Sheldon's First Industry

In *1879*, New York City businessman **JOHN H. ISELIN** and his brother **HARRY** built a flour mill in Sheldon, Iowa. The **PRAIRIE QUEEN FLOUR MILL** was located on the Milwaukee Railroad. As the mill was being constructed, **Iselin** built a company town south of the mill. This company town, on south third avenue, was called **ISELINVILLE**.

In *1890* the mill was sold to **SCOTT LOGAN** and by *1907*, Logan had the mill running to its greatest capacity, about 350 barrels a day.

As the production of wheat declined in Northwest Iowa, grain was shipped in from South Dakota, making flour more expensive.

By *1927* time ran out for the **PRAIRIE QUEEN MILL** and it closed. The mill closed because "the machinery wore out, the millers wore out and the flour was too good to compete, on a cost basis, with that milled by the big mills."

The **Prairie Queen Mill** sat empty for a few years, burning down in *1932*.

Brands sold included such names as "Prairie Queen",, "Big Four", "Bells of St. Mary's (for the Catholic customers),"Spotlight" (for the elevator customers), "Jersey Cream", and others.

Scott Logan purchased the Prairie Queen Mill in 1890 from the Iselins, remodeled it, installed a new roller system, bought the Big Four Mill, and operated both mills until the early 1920s, when wheat was no longer a profitable crop grown in Northwest Iowa. The mill closed in 1929. The pride of Sheldon was vacant until it was destroyed in two hours by the fourth major Sheldon fire on Sunday, April 10, 1932.

Scott Logan Milling Company had purchased the Big Four in 1890 and continued using the Big Four's label on its products, such as pancake flour. The Big Four got its name from Lyon, Sioux, O'Brien, and Osceola Counties.

3¾ POUNDS - NET WEIGHT - WHEN PACKED

BIG 4

BIG 4

SELF - RISING PANCAKE FLOUR

INGREDIENTS:-Wheat and Corn, Phosphate, Soda and Salt, Powdered Buttermilk.

MANUFACTURED BY

SCOTT LOGAN MILLING CO.
SHELDON, IOWA.

The Iselin brothers built what later became the Prairie Queen Mill, and the John H. Iselin Company dealt in many other businesses such as cattle, hogs, grain, produce, and consignments not only in Sheldon but also in New York and Chicago.

"What's wrong with Sheldon?" was a popular advertisement telling Sheldon residents they should buy Prairie Queen Flour at their grocery store, as it was a home product made in Sheldon.

3½ POUNDS   NET WEIGHT

Prairie Queen

CORN MEAL

MANUFACTURED BY
SCOTT LOGAN MILLING CO.
SHELDON, IOWA

When Nettie Minden Thill married Michael Thill in 1914, she took over her husband's business, called the Lunch Room, which was located in one room of his house west of the train depot. Nettie made and served delicious noon lunches and mid-morning and mid-afternoon snacks and coffee to railroad workers and passengers on the daily passenger trains, which totaled 18 a day at the peak. After 58 years of operation, the Lunch Room burned to the ground with many antiques lost in the fire.

The Scott Logan Milling Company manufactured cornmeal, and the Prairie Queen picture promoted that it was produced using top-quality cornmeal flour.

Margaret Fiebig, widow of Eugene Fiebig, opened Fiebig's Tavern on the south side of Ninth Street in Sheldon. It operated for many years, closing in 1979 to make way for a city parking lot.

A Mr. Highly of Storm Lake constructed a saloon that was the first brick building in Sheldon.

The Sheldon National Bank was established in 1905. William P. Iverson, vice president of the Union Bank, and his associates bought the controlling interest of the Sheldon National Bank from James F. Toy of Sioux City, and Iverson became president of the Sheldon National Bank. He was originally a druggist in Hudson, South Dakota.

When the Howard Hotel was built in 1888, it contained 35 rooms, but in 1911, it was remodeled, and there were 50 rooms, 18 having attached bathrooms. The Howard House is on the far right of this picture. Shipley Drug is on the left with a mortar and pestle monument outside.

The big rambling Sheldon House Hotel, on the northwest corner of Second Avenue and Ninth Street, was a mecca for all and headquarters for railroad travelers. The railroad encouraged its construction in 1873. The hotel was the largest and finest in Northwest Iowa. It stood on a large lawn across the street from the former location of the Chase Lumber Company. The last proprietors were Mr. and Mrs. F. Tescher. It brought $13,750 when it was sold at public auction, and it was ultimately razed.

This woodcut represents Sheldon in 1876. All but a small portion of the west part of town is in the picture. (Courtesy of D.A.W. Perkins.)

The Arlington Hotel was on the corner of Third Avenue and Tenth Street. It contained 54 rooms and a formal dining room that would seat 100 people. It later become a furniture store. Ultimately, it was burned by the Sheldon Fire Department during a controlled burn training fire.

Scott's Furniture & Undertaking sold furniture, rugs, window shades, upholstered furniture, and framed pictures. It also did repair work and was an undertaker.

F.W. Miller Clothing Store specialized in men's, boy's, and children's clothing with an emphasis on men's clothing and shoes.

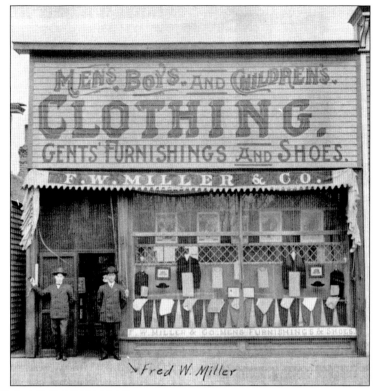

The McKeever Block, on the east side of Third Avenue, was built in 1901 and contained three sections. People's Clothing Store was in one of the three, with beautiful architectural characteristics and an engraved cornerstone dated 1935.

A.J. Schapp & Myers Land and Insurance handled real estate sales, insurance, and steamship tickets throughout Iowa, South Dakota, Minnesota, and the Gulf Coast.

The Red Owl Food Store sold groceries, including fruits, pop, and ice cream, and was on Third Avenue below the Royce Hotel. To promote more business, sales receipts were used for a drawing to give away a Chevrolet Deluxe Town Sedan to a lucky customer.

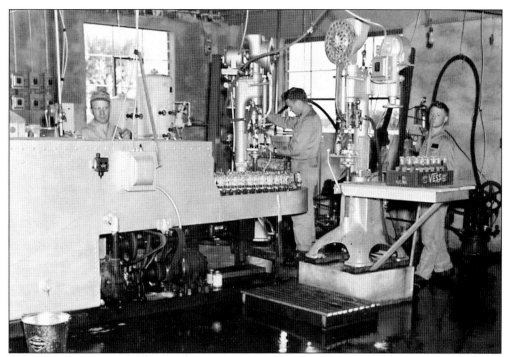

The Sheldon Bottling Plant, on the north side of Ninth Street, was founded in 1894 by Eugene Fiebig and was the largest pop distributor in the tristate area of Iowa, Minnesota, and South Dakota. When financial problems developed, it closed in 1936. The first noon whistle in Sheldon was the whistle on the top of the bottling works building.

The Curtis Candy Kitchen (1913) was opened by William Curtis. The fountain dispensers shown above are, from left to right, Bernice Speer, Ray Sweeny, and Gene Murray. It was a very popular fountain location for social gatherings. It served light lunches and had delicious homemade candy.

Jason Henry and his wife opened the Henry Café on the corner of Ninth Street and Third Avenue in 1925 but later changed the name to Corner Café. It was originally the Sleeper Brother's Union Bank, the second brick building constructed in Sheldon.

In 1946, the Sheldon Body and Fender Shop was operated by Messers. Feurstein and Whitsell. They also had a Hudson car dealership.

Washer Hardware was in the McKeever Block on the east side of Third Avenue. Roy Murphy opened Murphy's Store in this building in the late 1960s and sold men's shoes, clothing, work clothes, and accessories.

Since Sheldon was the center of a large trade area, the Starrett brothers traveled from Toulon, Illinois, and opened a department store in 1890 with three floors (including a basement) of items that carried "everything you might need," including groceries. The furnishings compared to large city stores. Due to a shortage of space, they later opened a men's clothing store called the White House Clothing Store on Ninth Street. This building had a white brick facade. The family operated the Starrett store for 68 years. During the Depression, they allowed payment for merchandise in the form of corn. In 1935, the store had 35 employees. When fire destroyed the business in 1958, the Starretts decided not to rebuild. Edward Starrett was president when it closed.

Ladies' clothing and millinery were located on the second story of Starrett's Department Store. Its motto was "The store that serves you better."

Shown is a Starrett Bros. advertisement for men's suits that appeared in the *Sheldon Mail* newspaper on February 10, 1919.

Originally Coomes Clothing, later Strak's Clothing, this men's clothing store sustained fire damage in the 1958 downtown fire. Strak's Clothing later became Tanner's Clothing in the same location.

Ellerbroek's was a ladies' ready-to-wear store next door to Starrett's on the west side of Third Avenue in downtown Sheldon where the 1958 fire started in the early morning hours.

A horse and wagon delivered milk products to homes until a motorized vehicle was purchased to replace it. Curtis Stone is pictured above.

The Iowa Theatre, formerly Sheldon Auto Company and a furniture and funeral parlor, was one of four theaters in Sheldon. It was established in June 1929 by Frank Kehrberg and his two sons. The first full-length sound feature was *The Rainbow Man*. The original two-story building was constructed in 1895 by Jewett Bros. of Sioux Falls, South Dakota, as a wholesale grocery warehouse. In the early 1900s, a third floor was constructed. The upper floor was a ballroom and meeting place for the Masons and other fraternal societies of Sheldon. It also housed Dr. Lloyd H. Mattice, Wolff and Whorley Law Office, and Mastbergen Jewelry. Later, it was converted to a combined Pizza Ranch, video arcade, and theater until a fire destroyed this beautiful building in 2002.

The Sheldon Motel was on the west edge of Sheldon on Highway 18. There were 30 units with air-conditioning, dial phones, and large desks for traveling salesmen.

The Daniels Motel was one block east of Sheldon City Park on Highway 18. The modern motel had 12 units. The 14th issue of the *Mobil Travel Guide*, the nation's best-known national travel guidebook, qualified the Daniels Motel for a listing.

Edwin P. Messer owned the hardware store in Sheldon for many years. He was known as a town booster, a member of the Grasshoppers baseball team, a civic leader, and a city councilman. His beard and his straight statue were very impressive. He can be seen here on the front steps of the store. Messer was a Civil War veteran. D.A.W. Perkins's law office was on the second floor of this building.

The First National Bank was organized on February 8, 1888, in the Frisbee Livery Barn. George W. Schee was president, and directors included Frank Frisbee and John Archer. The bank prospered and in 1922 was said to have been the largest bank in O'Brien County. It later became known as Security State Bank and was located in the present Northwestern Bank building.

Lambert Levering started a blacksmith shop that was later operated by G. Roetman. The blacksmith shop did general blacksmithing and horseshoeing. Horses played an important part in Sheldon residents' lives as their mode of transportation in the early days.

Ron Drenkow Motors was a Chrysler, Plymouth, and Dodge car dealership established in 1965. It was first located at the corner of Washington Avenue and Highway 18 and moved to Highway 60 east of Hill's Park. Later, Drenkow Motors purchased the Ken Karr Ford, Mercury Inc. car dealership and combined the dealerships, moving to an East Highway 18 location.

C. Van Dam Skelly Service Station carried a complete line of oil products and an up-to-date lubrication department on the corner of Ninth Street and Washington Avenue from 1920 to 1945. It was later a Standard Oil station operated by Tony Koerselman, Les Van Beek, and Al Mouw from 1927 to 1977. The building was most recently purchased by Joe Tokheim for classic car restoration.

A gas station with a coffee bar at the intersection of Highway 18 and Highway 60 became a popular gathering and social center for farmers and other Sheldon residents to discuss the latest happenings over a cup of coffee. In 1952, an explosion and fire in this building resulted in it being rebuilt, and it continued as Keen Corner until 1987, when it was acquired by Kum & Go Convenience Store and later Casey's General Store.

Council Oak, a branch of Tollerton & Warfield, purchased property to construct a new, modern supermarket on the corner of Third Avenue and Tenth Street. The new store had the finest in modern refrigeration, including fruit and vegetable counters as well as a fresh meat section. The new store was self-serve. The new store also had a free parking lot.

Farmers joined together to form a cooperative and bought the Button Elevator property in 1910. They called it the Farmers Co-Op Elevator. In 1941, they built their first cement grain storage silo. Sheldon also had a cooperative creamery that was established in 1919 and shipped 200,000 pounds of butter out in a year. In March 1960, no. 2 corn sold for $1.04 and soybeans at $2.34 a bushel.

Due to a shortage of workers in 1944, Swanson's Super Market was not able to hire help to carry out groceries, but its everyday low prices helped customers to save more on their food budgets, and the store gave customers S&H Green Stamps. After closing time on May 4, 1967, a fire started in the store, and by 11:30 p.m., the store and contents were a total loss. The building was owned by Mrs. Richard Myers Smith of Prospect Heights, Illinois. Al Swanson of Cherokee owned the business. It was located at Third Avenue and Eleventh Street. The loss was estimated at $275,000.

The first issue of the *Sheldon Mail* was January 1, 1873, when D.A.W. Perkins was editor and the town's population was 30 people. "The Paper's Out" was the headline, with the quote "We don't believe in that timorous and cowardly style of journalism, where the power behind the throne is afraid of its own shadow. An honest, conscientious, and fearless expression upon matters of the day is the only safe and successful course." The *Sheldon Mail* is now operated by the Wagner family as Iowa Information Publications.

Montgomery Ward was a national retail and mail-order catalog store on the west side of Third Avenue that competed with Sears and Roebuck. The 5,000-square-foot building contained furniture, clothes, tools, appliances, housewares, and more. It operated in Sheldon for over 50 years. It is now Downtown Hardware.

Ole Molmen started in the dairy business in 1919 when he purchased Scott Logan's Eastside Dairy. From 1919 to after World War II, it was called the Sheldon Dairy. After the war, it was called Molmen's Dairy. Well's Dairy of LeMars purchased the dairy in 1962. Pictured are John De Hoogh (left) and Curtis Stone (right).

In 1922, Henry Perrott moved from Hospers, Iowa, to Sheldon and opened Perrott Auto Repair at 804 Eighth Street. Upon his sudden death in 1946, his son Vincent assumed ownership. The business was relocated in 1959 to the Skelly Station at the corner of Eighth Street and Third Avenue, where gasoline, auto repair, radiator repair, and tire services were offered. The business transitioned to Perrott's Sales and Service in the late 1960s and became an outdoor power equipment sales and service center. (Courtesy of Dr. David Perrott.)

Arlan Van Wyk started his trucking business in 1958 in Sheldon with two trucks transporting goods. His brother Dennis joined him one year later but sadly died in an accident on March 13, 1988. The business has continued to grow under Arlan's leadership to a fleet of over 200 trucks on the road traveling all over America. Its motto is "We deliver peace of mind!" (Courtesy of Dave Van Wyk.)

In 1931, Neal Chase moved to Sheldon to open the Neal Chase Lumber Co. Chase had been manager of a lumber company in Petersburg, Nebraska. His knowledge of the building trades gave people confidence to purchase his products. Chase Lumber Co. has been a successful family business through the years in Sheldon. The business now operates in nearby cities with four additional lumberyards as Neal Chase Lumber Co. (Courtesy of Jane DeBates.)

Aalf's manufactured blue jeans for Gap, Levi Straus, J.C. Penney, County Seat, and Edwin's Blue Jeans from 1951 to 1999, when it closed and the building was left vacant. First, it was located on Highway 60 in the former Western Grocery Company building. Aalf's moved its operation to a newly constructed modern building on Sixteenth Street and Western Avenue in 1974.

Security State Bank opened in the 1920s in the Frisbee Bank Building. Gus Schneider and his son Claire traveled by train to Sheldon from Madison, Wisconsin, to explore opening the bank. Upon opening, Claire became vice president and Gus became president. Beginning capital was $65,000, a small sum by today's standards. Interest on savings accounts was set at four percent, and the loan rate was eight percent. In 1970, Richard Schneider, Claire's son, served as president. He retired in 1995, at which time the bank was purchased by Security National Bank of Sioux City, Iowa.

Citizens State Bank was organized after the Sheldon National Bank closed in 1961. J.L. Campbell Jr. of Humboldt, Iowa; Keith Campbell of Des Moines, Iowa; and Robert Dixon of Rolfe, Iowa, were instrumental in starting the new bank. It had Sheldon's first time and temperature sign. Citizens became very successful, but the location was limited, and a new bank was built on Third Avenue and Eighth Street to serve its customers.

Bob Hoogeveen and Dr. Ken Fertig had a vision to develop Village Northwest Unlimited, an adult residential handicapped facility, with the financial assistance of philanthropist Dick Wansink and many other community donors. The organization has grown nationally and is recognized as a premier provider of services to people with intellectual and developmental disabilities, autism, and traumatic injuries, serving its residents with privacy, dignity, and purpose.

Rosenboom Machine and Tool was founded in 1974 as a tool and die shop by Lary and Vivian Rosenboom. The company manufactures custom-crafted hydraulic cylinders for almost all applications. The company has an industry reputation for attention to detail and an honest approach to customer service. Rosenboom Machine and Tool has facilities in Sheldon, Iowa; Spirit Lake, Iowa; Bowling Green, Ohio; Yantai, China; and Shanghai, China. The company employs approximately 300 individuals in Sheldon.

On Thursday, March 6, 1958, at approximately 9:00 a.m., the sixth major fire, and the worst one of all, began in Ellerbroek's Women's Clothing Store. A faulty electrical switch started the fire and caused it to rush through the underground hallway and upstairs into the main room.

Ellerbroek's fire spread to the 62-year-old Starrett's Department Store, and the Arlington Annex, with Hedy's Café on the street level and apartments on the upper level, was engulfed in flames. Fire chief Zane "Zip" Hudson called for help, and 14 nearby towns responded, with a total of 220 firefighters available to fight the fire for 36 hours. When Zip was asked where the volunteer firemen came from, he said, "They came from every-which-a-way." The loss was estimated at $500,000.

These Sheldon firemen are dressed in their formal attire with hat and neckties, but they would not have arrived at a fire with this type of clothing when they were risking their lives trying to control a burn.

During the 1958 downtown fire, Sheldon contractor Jack Andringa climbed the building and rescued elderly Eleanor Gibson, bedridden due to illness, from a third-floor apartment in the Arlington Annex with the assistance of Al Dykstra and J.A. Vander Ploeg.

At 5:55 p.m. on June 4, 1968, Vogel Tire, formerly Bray Motor Company, was the eighth major fire in Sheldon, and approximately 100 firefighters and 50 volunteers battled this giant blaze. Within 30 minutes, Vogel Tire was demolished and the flames had traveled to the Armour Egg and Poultry Company. Dense black smoke from burning tires could be seen for miles. Firefighters spent 24 hours trying to contain the fire at Armour. The entire block burned to the ground. Vogel Tire rebuilt on the site and later sold the new structure to Gary and Barbara Rosenboom, who have operated Rosenboom Body Shop and Tire Sales since 1975.

This old brick building was demolished in 1956, and Hickman Standard Service Station replaced it that September with two service stalls, a four-pump gas capacity, a product display area, and an office. It was located on the corner of Third Avenue and Eleventh Street.

Three

CHURCHES AND HOUSES

God's word has been Sheldon's great heritage for the past 150 years. Spiritual needs are currently being served by 13 churches of various denominations, including Bethel Reformed Church, St. Patrick's Catholic Church, First Christian Reformed Church, Parkview Assembly of God, St. Paul Lutheran Church, Sheldon United Methodist Church, First Reformed Church, Calvary Baptist Church, Sheldon Church of the Brethren, Immanuel Christian Reformed Church, Living Water Community Church, Our Savior Lutheran Church, and United Pentecostal Church.

In less than six weeks after the railroad arrived, a Congregational church was organized. The church was incorporated on January 29, 1874.

St. Patrick's Catholic Church was the second church built in Sheldon, and the congregation's first church was erected in 1880. The present church was built in 1911 by Geiger Construction Company of Sheldon. The Methodist church was the third congregation to build and organize and held its services at Sheldon Junction. It officially started in 1873, with the first church being built in September 1881. St. Paul Lutheran Church began in 1878, and the church carried the German language at services into the 1900s. In 1922, under the pastorship of Rev. Henry Flentje, the second St. Paul church was constructed, a brick building on the corner of Tenth Street and Eleventh Avenue. The church is now occupied by Calvary Baptist Church. St. Paul Lutheran Church erected a new building in 1960 on Pleasant Court Drive. On April 23, 1895, the First Reformed Church organized. Services were initially held in the Adventist church. In 1899, a church was erected on the corner of Washington Avenue and Seventh Street. Bethel Reformed Church was organized in 1947, and a new sanctuary was built in 1952. The First Christian Reformed Church was organized in 1906 with 17 families. The congregation worshiped in the Adventist church, then the Baptist church that existed at that time, and later the Church of Christ. A small church building was erected on the corner of Eighth Street and Eleventh Avenue in 1907. In 1911, it was enlarged, and in 1951, a new church was constructed on the same site as the previous church. The Sheldon Church of the Brethren is a rural church with an interesting history starting in 1884 with several families from Illinois. Parkview Assembly of God, formerly known as Gospel Tabernacle, was organized in the 1930s. It is located across from Sheldon City Park and is affiliated with the Assembly of God Church.

Benjamin Jones built the first house in Sheldon. It stood on the corner of Third Avenue and Eleventh Street. The 1872 cornerstone is intact and on display in the Sheldon Prairie Museum. James Wycoff built the second home, on the corner of Ninth Street and Fourth Avenue. It was removed to make way for a municipal parking lot. A beautiful home was built by C.L. Soyster at 620 Fourth Avenue. A condominium now occupies this lot. Scott Logan, owner of the Prairie Queen Mill, built his home at the corner of Sixth Street and Sixth Avenue across from Sheldon City Park. It exists today at this location. Early resident H.C. Lane built his home at 724 Sixth Avenue in 1903. It is presently the Vander Ploeg Funeral Home. The Frisbee family of Wisconsin built numerous large homes, as did attorneys T.E. Diamond and G.C. Murray, in the east part of Sheldon. At the time they were built, the area on Tenth Street was known as Knob Hill.

The First Reformed Church was the official name for the church that was organized in April 1895. It held services in the Dutch language, despite the governor of Iowa making it illegal to use foreign language in Iowa churches. The first church building was dedicated on October 10, 1899, on the corner of Eleventh Street and Ninth Avenue. The second church was built in 1912, and the third church was constructed in 1939. The fourth church was dedicated on August 19, 1952, at its current location on Washington Avenue.

The Methodists held meetings in many places before they built their first church in Sheldon on the corner of Eighth Street and Fifth Avenue in 1881. A new brick sanctuary was built in 1899 and served the congregation until 1970. A new church was dedicated on October 27, 1978. For approximately eight years, the Methodists held their services in the United Congregational Church.

The first Catholic church met in the private home of Mike Burns. The second church built in Sheldon was completed in March 1880 on the corner of Ninth Street and Sixth Avenue. Due to windstorm, blizzard, and tornado damage, a new church was built in 1911 by the Geiger Construction Company at its present location on the corner of Fourth Avenue and Tenth Street.

The Congregational church was the first built in Sheldon, commencing in 1870. The congregation shared its church with the Methodists. The Congregational church held services in the morning, and the Methodists had their services in the evening until the Methodists built their own church in 1881. The Congregational church building later housed Sheldon's first children's day-care center. The church was razed to make room for a new theater.

The fifth church to be built in Sheldon was the wooden Baptist church in May 1884. In 1898, a new church was completed on the southeast corner of Seventh Avenue and Fifth Street. In 1961, Calvary Baptist Church purchased and moved into the former St. Paul Lutheran Church on Ninth Avenue and Tenth Street. The church was razed to make room for the Methodist parking lot.

The Christian Science church, also called First Church of Christ, Scientist, was organized in 1895 and bought the property at Fifth Avenue and Ninth Street and remodeled it. The membership became interested in the gospel of healing and regeneration. It later became the site of the Sheldon police station, city jail, and magistrate's court.

The First Christian Reformed Church was organized in 1906 and met in several other churches until a church was constructed on the northeast corner of Ninth Street and Ninth Avenue. It was remodeled and enlarged in 1911.

The First Christian Reformed Church built a new church in 1953 when the congregation outgrew its old church. In 1947, a committee was formed to study a new church. Ground-breaking was held on Thanksgiving Day 1952, and the cornerstone was laid on May 14, 1953. The new church was located on Ninth Street and Ninth Avenue. The cost of the new church was $950,000.

When the Lutheran congregation moved into its new church on Pleasant Court and Garfield Avenue in 1960, Calvary Baptist Church purchased the old Lutheran church. The Baptists met as a Bible study group in the Community Building before they acquired their new church structure.

The First Reformed Church was organized in 1895 and met in the church of Seventh-day Adventists until First Reformed built its own brick church and bought a parsonage in 1899. In 1966, it bought the property across the street to the east, built a parsonage, and used the previous parsonage as a youth house. The church added a fellowship and education wing in 1972.

In 1875, the First Congregational Church was organized in a primitive building about a mile and a half south of Sheldon. In 1875, the congregation built the first church in Sheldon. Erected between Tenth and Eleventh Street on Fifth Avenue, it served the congregation for 30 years.

BETHEL REFORMED CHURCH
SHELDON, IA.   13B

Bethel Reformed Church was organized in 1947 and met in the Community Building. In 1948, the congregation met in the new church basement. The home of a pioneer businessman, Joseph Shinski, was torn down to make way for a new church. Shinski was mayor in 1888 and justice of the peace. The new church was built using volunteer labor. This church was recently demolished to make way for a new church on the original school block location.

The Immanuel Christian Reformed Church was organized in 1972, but the new church was not erected until 1975 using a combination of wood and brick. This modern, attractive church was built on the corner of East Sixth Street and Union Avenue, near East Lawn Cemetery.

The first Sheldon Gospel Tabernacle was organized in the 1930s. Its name was changed to Parkview Assembly of God. The church is on Fourth Avenue west of Sheldon City Park.

St. Paul Lutheran Church began in 1878, and in 1954, the congregation chose the name St. Paul Lutheran Evangelical Church. A frame building was erected in 1893, but in 1921, a brick structure was constructed to replace it on the corner of Ninth Avenue and Tenth Street. In 1955, it purchased property on Pleasant Court. A parsonage was built in 1957, and in 1960, a new church was built on the corner of Pleasant Court and Garfield Avenue.

The First Church of the Brethren is located a short two miles north of Northwest Iowa Community College on Marsh Avenue and was organized in 1884. The congregation met in barns, sheds, schoolhouses, and open groves until the first church was constructed in 1894; it was remodeled in 1978.

The first and oldest house in Sheldon was built by Benjamin and Margaret Jones at 301 Eleventh Street. The basement was started in 1871 but not completed until 1872. Benjamin Jones was in the lumber business a half-block south of the house. In 1978, Dr. Earl Martin bought the house and converted it into a chiropractic office. The 1872 cornerstone is located in the Prairie Queen Museum in Sheldon.

On the southeast corner of Sixth Street and Sixth Avenue stands the historic house that Scott Logan built on four lots in 1902. He spent time trimming the trees across the street before it was Sheldon City Park. Logan purchased the Prairie Queen Mill and later the Big Four Mills.

James, Frank, and Fred Frisbee, influential in Sheldon's growth, moved from Wisconsin to Sheldon and built mansion homes like this one at 906 Tenth Street. Most small towns have lost their large houses, but Sheldon still has the beautiful homes that the Frisbees, H.C. Lane, and Scott Logan built in the early 1900s.

Fred E. Frisbee, a wealthy banker, built this three-story mansion in 1917 for his wife, Mame, and their three children, and they called their home Fairhill. The historic mansion was sold to Rudolph Longshore in 1940 and sectioned off into apartments in the 1940s.

T.E. Diamond was a prominent Sheldon attorney who built this home at 1142 Tenth Street. The home was designed and built by Beuttler & Arnold Architects of Sioux City, Iowa. It was considered one of Sheldon's most beautiful homes. The home was concrete with an open veranda, small porches, third-floor servant quarters, library space, and the latest decor.

The First Reformed Church and the First Christian Reformed Church consistories agreed that a home for the aged should be purchased. In 1926, the home of Dr. W.H. Myers was purchased for $12,000. It later became the Holland Home for the Aged until it expanded with several brick additions. The original home for the aged was moved to the country north of Sheldon on County Line Road and is currently owned by Craig and Donna Hoadley.

Robert Aborn, the grandson of Israel Sheldon (who gave Sheldon its name), worked at the Union Bank in Sheldon and built a house on the south end of town that overlooked Iselinville's cabins. It was surrounded by many trees but has since been razed. In 1938, cabins were built near the Aborn house with a modern Standard Oil service station with a lunchroom. The new service station was operated by George B. Evans. It was later owned by Louis Hollander. Foundations were laid for eight cabins in the beautiful Aborn grove on the service station property. It was one of the most attractive service stations and cabin sites in the country.

H.C. Lane's home at 724 Sixth Avenue is now Vander Ploeg Funeral Home. H.C. Lane arrived in Sheldon in 1871, a year before the railroad came in 1872. He operated the first lumber store in Sheldon. H.C. Lane could be called a Sheldon town father. He was a major force in the city's commercial growth.

C.S. Soyster built his home at 620 Fourth Avenue with an elegant tower, popular in many houses at the time. A guest of the Soyster home was William Jennings Bryan, who was a speaker at the annual meeting of the Sheldon Chamber of Commerce.

The home of W.N. Strong at 637 Fourth Avenue was built in 1874. He was the clerk of court for one term and accumulated large amounts of real estate. Strong had a lumber business in Sheldon.

This beautiful Colonial home was built by attorney George C. Murray. It is located on Tenth Street in the area known in the 1940s as Knob Hill. Danish immigrant wood workers completed all the intricate woodwork and lived in a large tent on the property during construction.

L.N. Wilsey built the Wilsey Flats, composed of six apartments with basements, at the corner of Third Avenue and Eighth Street in 1920. Each apartment had a kitchen, dining room, living room, two bedrooms, a bathroom, and a large closet.

Beautiful elm trees formed an arch over Sheldon streets providing shade. This view is looking east to the intersection of Ninth Street and Washington Avenue. Dutch elm disease wiped out most of the beautiful trees in the 1960s and 1970s.

Four

PEOPLE AND PLACES

Sheldon applied for a grant of $10,000 from Andrew Carnegie to build a library. The town received the last grant awarded by Carnegie for the building of a free public library. A unique feature of the library is the interior dome. All other Carnegie libraries had exterior domes that leaked, and the domes had to be removed. The Carnegie library became the Sheldon Prairie Museum in 1972 and is governed by the Sheldon Historical Society and Sheldon Prairie Museum Boards.

Sheldon was the residence of many knowledgeable businessmen who were instrumental in getting the town off to a good commercial start. Edwin Y. Royce, a visionary, was elected mayor and was responsible for the city's water and sewer systems. He constructed the Royce Hotel in 1880 and started building the Royce Opera House in 1893. The opera house had three stories. The first story featured businesses in the front of the building, and the front of the upper two stories had hotel rooms that opened onto two balconies and a huge stage. Unfortunately, the opera house was condemned for safety reasons.

The first post office was built in 1872. Trains brought the mail to Sheldon, and a horse-drawn wagon met the train and delivered the mail to the post office. Mail was delivered twice a day to Sheldon's city residences, or people could pick their mail up at the post office. The post office became a social and gossip center. Jack Donohue began rural delivery in 1914 with his horse-drawn wagon. The first postal rate was 2¢. In 1959, the trains discontinued mail delivery, and trucks begin delivering the mail to post offices. Zip codes commenced in 1966.

After Cram Hospital came Myers Hospital, which was renamed Good Samaritan Hospital. The Sheldon Community Memorial Hospital was built and opened in 1952 and is known today as Sanford Hospital.

When the Carnegie Public Library outgrew its building, a new brick public library was constructed on the corner of Fourth Avenue and Tenth Street, just east of the Carnegie building. Additional space was available to house many books and other educational materials.

Sheldon replaced the old armory with a new one in 1935 constructed by the Henry Geiger Construction Company of Sheldon at a cost of $88,000, with the Public Works Administration providing $39,645 and the City of Sheldon providing the balance. The new Community Building was Northwest Iowa's most popular convention headquarters and the center of community social and commercial activity for many years. The Community Building was remodeled by Uittenbogaard Construction in 1997.

Drs. Will, Lynn, and Judson Myers built a brick hospital on the corner of Pleasant Court and Garfield Avenue where the Lutheran church now stands. It was called Myers Hospital from 1920 until 1934. It was common practice to name the hospital after the doctor who operated it. It later became the Good Samaritan Hospital. The hospital was replaced in 1952. The Good Samaritan Hospital was razed, and the bricks from it were used to build two duplexes on Highway 18 west of the existing hospital. It became the site of the new Lutheran church in 1960.

Dr. W.H. Myers is pictured at his desk in his medical office above the Sheldon State Bank on the corner of Third Avenue and Ninth Street.

The first hospital in Sheldon was the F.W. Cram Hospital. It operated in a house west of the Community Building until it was moved to a larger house on the corner of Ninth Street and Fifth Avenue, where it was equipped with 10 beds and an operating room, with two nurses on duty.

The first water tower was built west of the Fourth Avenue fire station to supply water for Sheldon residents and to fight fires. Located at the base of the water tower were public restrooms and a city jail.

Benjamin and Margaret Jones, who built the first house in Sheldon, are pictured with their daughters, Nellie (first row) and Margaret (second row), and son, Frank.

The Sioux City & St. Paul Railroad received a land grant from the federal government to extend its railroad tracks to Sioux City, but it stopped at Le Mars. When Jimmy Griffin made this discovery, he filed homestead rights to 80 acres of the land grant in the east part of Sheldon adjacent to Eighth Avenue. He took his case all the way to the US Supreme Court to successfully obtain the rights to the homesteaded land.

A team of horses pulls a wagon of supplies in front of the *Sheldon Mail* office and the Corner Café around the 1920s.

Iceman William "Bill" Minden delivered ice with a horse-drawn wagon to owners of iceboxes and gave children slivers of ice, candy, and suckers. Bill Minden's funeral had the largest attendance ever in Sheldon with an unsurpassed number of flowers and mementos contributed by the children.

This 1909 Buick belonged to E.B. Myers's father, Dr. William Myers. Pictured above are his two brothers, Dr. Lynn L. Myers (left) and Dr. Judson Myers (back seat). Seated in the front left passenger seat is a cousin, Grace Richards. Dr. William Myers came to Sheldon in 1909, when Ed Myers was five years of age. Owners of these cars raced between Sheldon and Sanborn, reaching speeds of 40 miles per hour.

A 1908 photograph shows Sheldon postal workers in front of White's Hall. In 1878, Daniel S. White Jr. came from New Jersey. He wanted to build a new store in Sheldon, the largest one between Sioux City and Mankato, upon the condition he could buy the corner lot. The building later became Hollander's 5-10-25 Cent Store and is now a dental office. A part of the building became a post office before the post office was built on the corner of Fourth Avenue and Eighth Street in 1935.

An architect's rendering shows the new post office at 801 Fourth Street in 1935. The cornerstone provides the following information: Henry Morgenthau Jr., secretary of the Treasury; Louis A. Simon, supervising architect; Neal A. Melick, supervising engineer; and James A. Farley, postmaster general. The cost of the new post office was $50,000.

Edwin Royce's dream was to build a three-story opera house as a center for arts and entertainment with a seating capacity of 2,000 and hotel rooms for guests on the south side of Ninth Street at Third Avenue. Construction took 10 years. It was condemned before it was opened for business due to safety problems and took four months to be demolished in 1907.

After the death of Margarete Jones's husband, Benjamin, she donated the north half of her lot, where the first house in Sheldon was built, to the Masons, who built the Masonic temple in 1915.

The Sheldon Community Memorial Hospital opened in 1952 with 25 beds and facilities to care for six newborn babies. Since opening, it has been remodeled and updated many times, with an added clinic attached. In the hospital dedication program was written the following: "Erected for the welfare of the people, through the generosity and cooperation of public-spirited residents, past and present, of this community; a structure dedicated to the alleviation of human suffering to the relief of ills that beset man and to the glory of a new life."

HOTEL - ROYCE,

N. RICHARDS, Proprietor.

EASTER SUNDAY, 1896.

MENU.

Consomme Royal
Cream Slaw

Spanish Olives   New Radishes
Boiled Fresh Haddock ala Nelson
Pommes Hollendaise

Lettuce   Chow Chow
Boiled Philidelphia Ham,
                              Spanish Sauce

Steamed Potatoes
Roast Prime Ribs of Beef au Jus
Mashed Potatoes   June Peas
Spring Lamb, Mint Sauce
Sugar Corn   Stewed Tomatoes
Domestic Duck Stuffed, Currant Jelly

Easter Eggs en Tartar

Escolloped Oysters Ala Maryland
Fricassee of Chicken Au Petit Pois
Tymbals of Cranberries with Whipped Cream

Shrimp Salad

Apple Pie   Lemon Meringue Pie   Hot Mince Pie

Strawberry Short Cake
Delmonico Ice Cream
Assorted Cake
Angels Food
Raisins
Nuts
Fruit
Cheese and Crackers

Cafe Noir

The Royce Hotel was built in 1890 by E.Y. Royce on Ninth Street. The ground floor had a fancy restaurant with excellent food, and there were 40 hotel rooms. Pictured is the Easter Sunday 1896 menu from the hotel under proprietor N. Richards.

Sheldon resident Connie VerHoef was chosen as Miss Iowa at the Surf Ballroom in Clear Lake, Iowa, in 1953. She went on to Atlantic City as one of the 52 finalists in the annual Miss America Pageant.

Five

FAMOUS BANK EMBEZZLEMENT

It was a cold day on January 16, 1961, when the first customer arrived at the Sheldon National Bank to make an early morning deposit. A sign posted on the door stated: "This Bank Closed by Order of the Board of Directors M.D. Moon, National Bank Examiner in charge."

Soon word of the bank embezzlement was circulating in the community, and residents were in shock that the Sheldon National Bank closed its doors, never to reopen. The bank president's daughter, 58-year-old Burnice Iverson Geiger, had been employed at the bank for 38 years and was its assistant cashier for more than a decade. She confessed to embezzling the staggering sum of $2,126,859—one of the largest amounts ever embezzled in banking history in the United States. The bank, the oldest in Sheldon, had been established in 1905 and was capitalized at $50,000.

While Sheldon residents were absorbing the startling news, scores of newspaper reporters, photographers, and television and radio stations descended on the city of 4,663 residents. Calls were made to the *Sheldon Mail* office from Chicago, New York, Boston, and Philadelphia news services. The news even reached international proportions. Reporters from *Life* magazine came to Sheldon. Upon investigation by the bank examiners, it was discovered that Burnice operated two sets of books in her basement office. In her time as a bank employee, Burnice never took a day off from work. She could not take the chance her secret would be discovered, even though her basement office always remained locked.

Burnice pled guilty to 35 counts of embezzlement and misappropriation of bank funds and was sentenced to 15 years in federal prison in Alderson, West Virginia. She was released after six years of incarceration and returned to Sheldon to live with her elderly parents. Burnice lived a very quiet life upon her return until her death on October 25, 1981, at 78.

Another chapter in the story and what some believe to be Burnice Geiger's downfall was the arrival of Harold Kistner in Sheldon with Feed Bio-Zyme, a feed supplement made by his company, the Northern Biochemical Corporation (NBC). Burnice became a stockholder, and the business grew fast, with 45 new cars, 3 twin-engine airplanes, and 126 employees. Kistner's demise came when the bank closed. Most interesting is the fact that Elliot Roosevelt, son of the late president Franklin D. Roosevelt, had been hired by NBC as the company's financial advisor. Roosevelt remained in Sheldon, as he believed the company had a great future, and worked to find investors, but the company failed. Kistner was sentenced to eight years in prison on counts of fraud and conspiracy to aid and abet Burnice Geiger.

Burnice Iverson attended Sheldon High and graduated in 1920. She participated in high school plays with Wallace Geiger, who was a year younger. After graduation, she went to the University of Colorado for one year and then returned to Sheldon to work in the bank where her father, William Iverson, was president. At 23, Burnice married her high school sweetheart, Wallace Geiger, at her parents' home on Thanksgiving 1925.

When Burnice Geiger was arrested for embezzlement, this picture of her sitting by the Christmas tree in her home was one of the only photographs that could be found. Pictures of Burnice were very rare.

When Burnice Iverson and Wallace Geiger were married, they received his parents' 1915 combination stucco and brick house at 918 Sixth Street as a wedding present and a gift of $10,000 to update the home. This home was built by Wallace's father, a former colonel and wealthy contractor who owned Geiger Construction Company of Sheldon.

The Sheldon National Bank was established in 1897, reorganized in 1905, and combined with the Union Bank in 1916 when William Iverson and his associates bought the controlling interest of the Sheldon National Bank from James F. Toy. Iverson served as an acting officer. He later became president of the bank until it was closed by the Federal Deposit Insurance Corporation in January 1961.

These blank checks were available to customers who had checking accounts with the Sheldon National Bank. They were known as counter checks and were available at merchants' cash registers to pay for merchandise.

THE SHELDON NATIONAL BANK

SHELDON, IOWA

January 16, 1961

THIS BANK CLOSED BY ORDER OF THE BOARD OF DIRECTORS.

M. B. Moon, National Bank Examiner, in charge

The notice that appeared on the front door of Sheldon National Bank on July 16, 1961, was signed by M.B. Moon, bank examiner. It was discovered that morning during a routine audit that Burnice Geiger had embezzled $2,126,859 over a 35-year period. It was one of the largest bank embezzlements in the United States at that time.

Sheldon National Bank depositors crowd around the teller window to claim and collect their money deposits from the closed bank. The Federal Deposit Insurance Corporation (FDIC) reopened the bank for depositors to claim their deposits. The FDIC insured accounts up to $10,000 in 1961.

After John Lode collected a check for the money in his bank account at the Sheldon National Bank, he appears pleased. On the first day the FDIC reopened the bank, 400 depositors were paid $573,307 to pay out their accounts.

Elliot Roosevelt (pictured at a press conference), son of Pres. Franklin D. Roosevelt, was hired by Harold Kistner Jr. of the Northern Biochemical Company to find the financing to restart NBC, as he believed in the company product, but he was unable to put together the financing needed to continue the business. Kistner was later sentenced to eight years in prison for being an accomplice of Burnice Geiger. She invested in NBC and provided bank funds to keep the business operating until the embezzlement was uncovered. NBC produced an enzyme in animal food that claimed to put weight on livestock with less feed.

Otto Bartz was president of the board of directors of the Sheldon National Bank. This picture portrays the board president's feeling of bewilderment with the Geiger embezzlement.

A collage of pictures depicting the embezzlement appeared in the *Sheldon Mail* and included Burnice's arrest picture, the bank closing note on the door, a Sheldon National Bank advertisement with the slogan "Bank with Confidence," and a cash register with a note attached to customers that no checks would be accepted from the Sheldon National Bank.

Pictured is Burnice's desk with her wooden swivel chair in the office where she kept records in the basement of the Sheldon National Bank. Her office was painted pink and green, her favorite colors. Burnice kept two sets of records for her depositors' accounts and kept an accurate account of her total embezzlement funds to the exact penny. She had the only key to the basement office and the only access to her books. Burnice never took a vacation or sick day from her work. Burnice stated to the bank examiners that she kept everything in longhand, as she did not like the newfangled accounting machines. She advised the examiners in January 1961, when they questioned a small discrepancy, "I give up—it will never balance." The FDIC audit confirmed her exact numbers.

Burnice Geiger is pictured after her arrest and appearance in federal court in Sioux City, Iowa.

Six

SHELDON SCHOOLS

A progressive educational spirit has been demonstrated by the patrons of the Sheldon Community School District thorough its 150-year history. The history of the school district is one of steady growth and academic achievement constantly striving for excellence in education. Many longtime Iowa educators and political figures (including US senators, governors, and Vice Pres. George H.W. Bush, who visited the school in 1987) have commented that they have never seen a more beautiful school campus and such well-maintained buildings. It has been said on many occasions over the years that there is not a school district complex in the state of Iowa that is more beautiful and well-planned than the Sheldon Community School District campus. It is a model for how to plan a school campus. The vision shown by the Sheldon school patrons, administrations, teachers, and boards of education over the years has afforded the students and everyone in the community the opportunity to enjoy these beautiful facilities on an unequalled school campus. The Sheldon Community School District states: "The mission of the Sheldon Community School District is to prepare all learners to be productive citizens." It is a mission the schools in the school district, serving the communities of Archer, Ashton, Matlock, and Sheldon, have performed with pride and distinction. In addition to the public schools, Sheldon also supports two outstanding private schools. St. Patrick's School was built in 1956, and Sheldon Christian School commenced in 1917. Both were built for K–8 instruction.

Sheldon looks with enthusiasm to the future and the coming needs and challenges to educate the children in the community. As Margaret Mead once said, "Never doubt that a small group of thoughtful, community citizens can change the world; indeed, it is the only thing that ever has."

In 1886, continued growth in enrollment required the addition of a second wing on the wooden two-story building.

In 1894, the first brick school was an elaborate building, said to be the finest in Iowa. Newspaper records indicate that "the square tower framing the South entrance is 80 feet high and at all times when school is in session the national flag may be seen floating over the same from all directions, over 100 feet above street level."

Pictured are W.I. Simpson and his faculty. His assistants, filling the various departments of instruction, were recognized as teachers possessing the highest qualifications.

Frank Bowne was the first Sheldon High School graduate in 1887.

On a bitterly cold day in January 1903, fire broke out in the heating vents of the school and spread quickly throughout the building. A cold, snowy day and frozen water mains hindered the firefighters. The school was a total loss.

An early Sheldon grade school classroom is pictured in 1912. Students are wearing knickers, hair ribbons, and button shoes. This is a first-grade class under the instruction of a Miss Kelly. The classroom was in the southeast corner of the basement of the old school, which was demolished in 1970.

Pictured is an early manual training classroom.

Pictured here is Sheldon's 1907 football team. Note the coach with a derby hat. Helmets were leather with little or no head protection. In the early days of football, teams traveled by train to the games. Sheldon was not in a conference until 1925, so games were scheduled according to the train schedule.

The 1910 Sheldon girls' basketball team is shown here.

The new school, built in 1903, changed in appearance through the years as the turrets were roofed over.

The first junior college was established in September 1926 and was attached to the south end of the existing high school. Supt. F.H. Chandler welcomed a group of 36 students. Tuition was $50 per semester. Enrollment was limited to 60 students. Sheldon Junior College closed in May 1943 when there was a shortage of teachers and students due to World War II. It reopened in a new facility in 1946 and continued until May 1951.

Pictured is the 1946 Sheldon High School football team, coached by Walt Olsen.

The Sheldon Junior College basketball team in 1927–1928 was known as the Jaysees. They were crowned the 1927 Junior College Champions of Iowa. From left to right are (first row) Evert Payne, Edward Pohlmann, John Gorzeman, Don Jinkinson, Earl Jinkinson, and Gilbert De Boer; (second row) Roy McKinney, Merrill Fritts, Dick McKay, Art "Babe" Roggen, Supt. F.H. Chandler, Fay Lamkuil, Lee Pierce, and George Sweeney.

The Sheldon Orabs captured the Lakes Conference title for the first time in the 1954–1955 boys' basketball season. From left to right are (first row) D. Kohnke, B. Mulder, R. Bauer, D. Johnson, and J. Turner; (second row) K. Pap, M. Oosterhuis, L. Landhuis, W. Van Meeteren, and B. Schneider; (third row) coach L. Uknes, manager T. Pape, G. Randall, R. Reisinger, manager J. Miller, and assistant coach L. Shortinghuis. The conference title would elude the Orabs for 41 long years before they again claimed the crown in 1996.

The first high school was built in 1916 to the west of the 1903 school, visible on the right side of the photograph. The gymnasium attached to the high school was built in 1934. The junior college was started in 1926 and was added on the south end of the existing high school.

The Sheldon High School marching band participated in the 1953 homecoming day parade in downtown Sheldon.

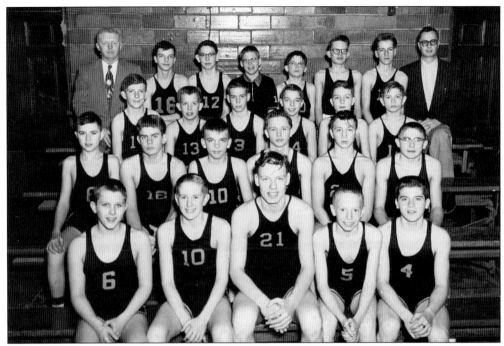

Pictured is 1957 boys' junior high basketball team. The Sheldon Orabs had a successful year with many fine athletes on this team.

Teenville was Sheldon's flourishing self-operated gathering place for teenagers, particularly on weekends. Students are improving their Fifth Avenue "home" through the cooperative efforts of its members by applying a coat of paint to the building.

By 68 percent, voters approved the 1956 construction of East Elementary with a total price tag of $251,556. The new school was opened in 1957, and the dedication of the building read: "Firm in the conviction that the public school is our nations bulwark and a basic essential of an effective democracy, the Sheldon Board of Education proudly dedicates this school to present and future generations of young Americans with the sincere hope that it will forever serve as a dynamic force in the perpetuation of liberty and enlightenment among free men."

Fire drills using the steel fire escape were common in the three-story elementary school building in the fall and spring.

This artist's drawing depicts the new Sheldon High School opened in 1969. This building, in excellent condition with up-to-date technology, continues to serve the needs of the Sheldon Community School District.

The 1920 Sheldon graduating class sponsored a contest to name their school annual, and eighth-grader Beth Powell won with Orab. She chose the name by combining the school colors, orange and black. It continues today to describe Sheldon students, athletic teams, and yearbooks. Sheldon students 102 years later are still enthusiastically supporting the home team, the Orabs. Sheldon has a long and proud history of its school name despite the fact that the *Des Moines Register*, in 1981, voted Sheldon's team name the worst in the state of Iowa.

St. Patrick's Church built St. Patrick's Elementary School south of the church on Fourth Avenue in 1956. The first teaching staff, who taught the Catholic religion and elementary education, were nuns from the Presentation Sisters of the Blessed Virgin Mary of Dubuque and Marguerite Wolf as a lay teacher.

The first Sheldon Christian School, with an emphasis on Christian education, was built in 1917 on Eighth Street with 40 children enrolled. A larger four-room brick school was built in 1949 south of the Christian Retirement Home. Later, four more rooms and a gymnasium were added.

In 1964, the Northwest Iowa Vocational School was founded as an experimental program of the Iowa Department of Public Instruction. During that time, students from 19 schools attended classes spread throughout downtown Sheldon. The initial board purchased a 146-acre farm located west of Sheldon, and construction began. Today, the school has invested in the students of Northwest Iowa and is known as Northwest Iowa Community College (NCC). It has 12,500 alumni, with a majority staying in the area to become valuable members of the workforce and community.

The new junior college addition onto the high school was established in 1926 and welcomed 36 students. Dean Margaret Burns explained to the students that the courses offered were the standard courses found in all colleges and universities in the United States. When the students graduated from two years in junior college, their credits would be accepted by all colleges in Iowa. Tuition was $45 per semester with an additional $5 chemistry fee.

Seven

MILITARY SERVICE

In 1898, Company E, 56th Regiment of the Iowa National Guard was headquartered in Hull, Iowa. A train loaded with Company E soldiers left Hull and passed through Sheldon, headed for Cuba to defend the United States from Spain.

After the Spanish-American War, Company E headquarters moved from Hull to Sheldon. Officers were chosen by election. Lieutenants were William "Bill" Bray and George Carpenter. The following year, W.H. Bailey was chosen to replace Bray and Carpenter. Jerome B. Frisbee was the first captain of Company E in Sheldon.

Capt. Jerome Frisbee drew the building plans for the gray-brick armory that stood where the Community Building stands today. Captain Frisbee solicited the funds to finance the $10,000 building.

When the United States declared war on Germany in 1917, Company E was divided into two units; one was sent to France as part of the Rainbow Division. The other was sent to the Mexican border for further training with the Sandstone Division.

In January 1918, a welcome arch was erected by the Sheldon Commercial Club on Third Avenue and Tenth Street from curb to curb. The arch reached 30 feet high at the peak and cost $550. The arch was lit with 60 incandescent lamps. A large eight-foot eagle spread over the top of the arch. The names of 284 Sheldon servicemen were placed under glass in the pedestals of either side of the arch. A huge service flag is displayed in the Sheldon Prairie Museum with their names hidden under the stars.

When the men of the Rainbow Division returned to Sheldon by train, they paraded under the Victory Arch to the armory and listened to a short address by Mayor E.L. Richards. The Iowa National Guard unit in Sheldon was reorganized and redesignated Company I, 133rd Infantry.

This was Sheldon's first armory on Ninth Street; it was razed, and a new Community Building that included an armory was constructed on the site. The new armory was adjacent to the H.S. Cobb residence on Ninth Street. It was the focal point of Sheldon sport and social activity and the headquarters of the National Guard and Company E soldiers. Sheldon High School played basketball here. There was a roller-skating rink in the winter, and public dances were popular. Sheldon High School graduation was held here until 1970.

Guardsmen from Northwest Iowa entered the Great War in September 1917 reporting for military duty. They headed by train to Deming, New Mexico, to begin military training. Some also went to New York.

The end of World War I was November 11, 1918, and Sheldon celebrated this event with a giant parade.

A welcome arch with a large spread eagle at the top was erected at the intersection of Third Avenue and Tenth Street by the Sheldon Commercial Club to honor World War I veterans in 1918. The arch reached from curb to curb with the veterans' names inside a lit case on each side of the arch.

SHELDON
EANERS
HATTERS

Sheldon townspeople closed their
businesses to watch Company I of
the Iowa National Guard, inducted
into the Regular Army, march
to the depot in February 1941.

World War I	**World War II**		**Vietnam**
Edward Cowie	Clarence Andringa	Wilmar Ten Kley	Harlan Brandts
Peter Faber	Elmer P Brinkman	Patrick B Lynch	Robert Brinkman
Frank Hopkins	Walter Brunhaver	James A Marmon	Akke Timmer
Henry Jansma	Wallace Bunker	John Pater	Alvin Van Riesen
Orley W. Klock	Robert Chapin	Richard Pater	
Carl McGlothlen	Clifford De Boer	Wayne Peterson	
Sylvester Michael Mulhern	Boyd Ellerbroek	John Letcher Propst	
John A Slothouber	Donald Gottertz	Walter Schmidt	
Fred Van Der Pol	Kenneth Heijn	Cullen Schroder	
	Joe Hof	John Shriver	
	Jack Steen Kelly	William Struyk	

This war memorial was erected to honor all the Sheldon veterans who gave the supreme sacrifice during the world wars and Vietnam.

Dick Kehrberg (left, chamber of commerce president) and Mayor L.A. "Hap" Houlihan (right) check home front donations in a Penny-a-Day can on a Sheldon street corner. The money was given to the federal government to buy arms. Sheldon received statewide publicity for the idea but little money.

Sheldon residents gather to say goodbye to local servicemen being deployed for service in World War II.

Leaving the Sheldon train station for World War II in 1941, Company I would later head to Ireland, closer to the war in Europe.

During World War II, men, women, and children canvassed farms and other areas for scrap iron for the war effort. This Starrett Bros. truck was loaded with old scrap iron that they were fortunate to find and donate for the war effort.

INVASION PRAYER SERVICES

The Allied invasion of the Axis European countries began Monday night.

Millions of our country's boys and men are in this invasion struggle, with sacrifices now unknown.

All Sheldon churches will hold a season of prayer tonight, Tuesday, starting at 8 o'clock.

All business places will close from 7:30 till 8:30. All church bells will ring at 7:30, 7:45 and 8 o'clock.

I know our people will realize the seriousness of the invasion movement and what it means, and will enter into this time of prayer with serious minds.

I hereby proclaim that the above hour be set aside for prayer.

MAYOR L. A. HOULIHAN

The Invasion Prayer Services were requested by Mayor L.A. Houlihan, who had this brochure distributed on all car windshields and to all businesses and churches.

A traditional Memorial Day parade takes place in Sheldon in 1960. The parade was led west on Ninth Street by American Legion commander Harold DeWaay. Memorial Day services have been held each year in Sheldon City Park or at Sheldon High School. The program recognizes all Sheldon residents who have served their country in the armed forces.

The four brothers of the Diekevers family all entered the war effort in World War II. They are, from left to right, Marvin "Fritz," Adrian "Rusty," George, and Harold "Pat."

Men and women volunteer to display the flags purchased by donors such as businesses, clubs, churches, veterans, and Sheldon residents. The Avenue of Flags has over 250 flags. The volunteers meet early in the morning to place the flags in Sheldon City Park. In 1988, Vice Pres. George H.W. Bush toured the Avenue of Flags on a campaign stop in Sheldon when he was running for president.

An American Legion recognition celebration is held at the end of World War II. The recognition of men and women who served took place in the Community Building after the conclusion of the Second World War. (Courtesy of Victor Scholten Jr.)

Eight

PARKS AND WEATHER

The Sioux City & St. Paul Railroad needed gravel for its roadbed in 1872 and was fortunate to locate gravel and sand pits near Sheldon. These pits eventually provided a playground for children and adults in what later became Hill's Park. Hill's Park is about a half-mile north of Sheldon on Old Highway 60. The hills are covered in wildflowers, grass, and trees and, thanks to the vision of Paul Woods, have become a park, playground, and campground. The Sheldon Trails Committee built an arch at the beginning of the bike/walking trail through the park.

After the railroad roadbeds were completed, sand from the pits was used to make bricks at a plant owned by Geyer and Glosser. At its peak, the company manufactured 25,000 bricks a day. These bricks were used to pave Sheldon streets in 1913.

The Sioux City & St. Paul Railroad donated land between Ninth and Tenth Streets and Third and Fourth Avenues for a park. The town fathers decided to sell lots for commercial buildings instead. The railroad directors became upset and rescinded their grant. They later donated a larger plot for the present Sheldon City Park.

The city needed a water tower and began digging its foundation in the park. When they reached the depth of 16 feet, they discovered a woolly mammoth tusk. Sheldon resident George Hudson, who had been digging, took the tusk home and hid it because he was afraid people would dig for other fossils in the park. After his death, his brother revealed the tusk at the Sheldon Centennial Celebration in 1972.

Sheldon City Park displayed two 1837 howitzer cannons from the US Army that weighed 1,200 pounds each. One was stolen, and the other was removed from the park and brought to the museum and placed on a specially built carriage.

Early settlers feared snowstorms as one of their greatest hardships. The severest blizzards occurred in 1871, 1872, 1873, 1880, 1881, and 1888. No lives were lost in the 1871 blizzard, but several deaths occurred in 1872 attributed to a lack of adequate warm clothing. The 1873 storm involved 22 pupils, ages 5 to 22, and 2 adults who were trapped overnight in a home used as a school. By 11:00 that evening, there was no heat. Two mattresses were shared by the 24 people using coats and blankets to cover themselves. By the next afternoon, they were finally able to return home. On October 6, 1880, a three-day snowstorm caused 15-foot drifts on the railroad tracks. Corn was still in the fields and coal was scarce, so corn was burned for heat. Late in the afternoon of January 12, 1888, one of Sheldon's worst blizzards began. The temperature dropped 60 degrees in 12 hours. One teacher kept her students in school, while another tied a rope around her students, and they walked to the nearest farm. Calvin Herd started home on his pony. His pony made it home, but he did not. William Bilsland and his two sisters were traveling home in a sleigh until the horses refused to move, even after trying to ride the horses. William dug a hole as shelter for his sisters and set out walking home, which took all night. The next day, the girls were found frozen to death.

The shaded Sheldon City Park has a shelter house and many tables for the picnic lovers who come from miles around on summer weekends, a ball diamond for baseball and softball, and playground equipment for the children. A swimming pool was also located in Sheldon City Park until it was moved near the high school in 1978. There are ample bleachers for watching events. A woolly mammoth tusk was found under the Sheldon water tower (shown in this picture). The tusk was discovered 16 feet below the surface and is on display at the Sheldon Prairie Queen Museum.

Sheldon's summer band platform, erected in July 1890, was constructed with wood. Many years of summer band concerts attracted crowds of music lovers, but it had to be taken down due to safety conditions and was never replaced.

Cram Athletic Field was first a fair grandstand on the west side of Sheldon, but the fairs died out, so Sheldon High School claimed it and played football games there until 1970. It was named after Dr. Fred Cram, a local doctor.

Jason Henry trained horses from the Sherwood Farm racetrack and raced sulky horses at the racetrack in the fairgrounds on Western Avenue. G.W. Sherwood introduced horse racing when he bought a farm, raised horses, and built a racetrack on his farm.

The Sheldon Country Club has a nine-hole course with many natural hazards and a clubhouse. Men's and women's leagues are scheduled during the summer months. The course is a par 36. The course record is 29, set in 1969 by Phillip Vander Ploeg.

Eli A. Smith, a US mail carrier, and his wolf team passed through Sheldon on a $10,000 bet on February 28, 1909. This was Eli Smith's return trip from Alaska with the wolf team. It is not known whether Smith and his team accomplished their goal, but one can imagine that they had many adventures trying. The large building in the right background was the Commercial College in Sheldon. (Courtesy of Vernon Hoy.)

Joe Ulveling, a pharmacist at the Rexall drugstore, volunteered to promote baseball by teaching youngsters the fundamentals and arranging and supervising games for them to play each summer. They were known as Pee Wees and Midgets. The young teams were sponsored by the American Legion. Each year, the Sioux City Soos minor-league team came to give young boys baseball instruction.

It took a lot of benches for spectators to watch baseball and other events at Sheldon City Park. A refreshment stand for pop and appetizing treats was a necessity by the ball diamond. The Boy Scouts operated the concession stand seen in the background.

This park, located a quarter of a mile from the intersection of Highways 18 and 60, has 11.5 acres of tree-covered mounds, a stone shelter house, restrooms, picnic tables, fireplaces, and electrical hookups for campers. The shelter house was a WPA project in 1938 and was restored in 2022 by a private donor gift.

The voter turnout in 1976 showed that 60.9 percent voted to build the indoor pool. It was built in 1978, but the circulation system, humidity problems, and a roof beyond repair caused the indoor pool to close its doors on Sunday, February 4, 2007.

112

The Izaak Walton League sponsored a yearly fishing day, called Kids' Fish Day, on the Floyd River north of Sheldon. Many prizes in each age category for catching fish were given to the young fishermen.

Many times, when Sheldon had unusual amounts of rain, the Floyd River flooded out of its banks. Record rainfalls came to Northwest Iowa on Sunday, June 7, 1953. Sheldon reported 8.58 inches of rain. By Monday, June 8, the Floyd River, swollen by these torrents of rain, smashed out of its banks, surging over large areas of Northwest Iowa with tremendous flooding.

A team of horses and several men were needed to rescue an automobile that slid into a curb and had no traction to move.

A customer on the way to breakfast at the popular L'Trio Grill had a narrow path to walk after a recent snowstorm.

Nature provided the beautiful snow scene in Hill's Park. The snow-covered hills enticed kids of all ages to bring their sleds or toboggans to slide down the hills.

In February 1936, Sheldon had 31 inches of snow with temperatures below zero 22 of the 29 days. Average snow for the whole winter was normally about 7 inches, but that winter the city had about 59 inches. According to Ross Forward, Sheldon's local weatherman for over 50 years, the city's all-time high temperature was July 7, 1936, at 108 degrees and all-time low temperature was -42 degrees on January 19, 1912.

Starrett's and all the other city business had to shovel their sidewalks due to a heavy snow on February 15, 1909, if they wanted customers to come and buy items from their stores.

The First Reformed ball team won the championship tournament among the many church city leagues in 1959 at the Joe Ulveling Baseball Field in Sheldon City Park. The First Reformed softball team won three championships in four years of play. From left to right are (first row) Lee Wissink (batboy), Clarence Hector, Elmer Den Hartog, Bernard Wissink, Ray Brandts, and Roger Vander Berg (manager); (second row) Arlan Boone, Les Douma, Gene Den Hartog, Harold Hector, and Jim Wolbrink.

Nine

Uptown of Iowa

Sheldon was platted by the Sioux City & St. Paul Railroad surveyors in the summer of 1871, a year before the railroad laid its last rail into the town. Sheldon is in Floyd Township, O'Brien County, Iowa. All land in Floyd Township came into private ownership through federal land grants. By January 1, 1873, Sheldon's population was 30 people.

The heart of the town of Sheldon, the business district, is located on Ninth Street and Third Avenue. Sheldon's slogan was "The Uptown of Iowa" given its location in the state.

The first train brought many carloads of lumber. Some of the lumber was designated for the railroad's depot. A Mr. Highly of Storm Lake was another recipient of the lumber, which he used to construct the first brick building in Sheldon.

H.C. Lane erected the next building for a lumber office. Lane started the first lumberyard. S.S. Bradley built the second lumberyard, and James Wykoff the third. W.A. Fife built a general store that was completed in late July 1872. Dan McKay, Joseph Walker and his son, and LeRoy Hackett did the carpentry work on Fife's general store. B.E. Bushnell built a hardware sore. D.A.W. Perkins, Sheldon's first lawyer, had a building for his law office. He wrote an extensive history of O'Brien County that is recognized as an excellent account of the county's early days. Benjamin Jones built the first warehouse and the first house as his residence.

By the fall of 1872, many other buildings had been constructed. The first issue of the *Sheldon Mail* newspaper was dated January 1, 1873. By this date, the following businesses were available in Sheldon: hotel, doctor, lawyer, restaurant, saloon, blacksmith, clothing, hardware, harness shop, grain buyer, general store, feed and coal dealer, farm machinery, grocery, and dry goods.

More carloads of lumber arrived, and 1873 was a progressive year with many businesses being built. Sheldon became the largest town in O'Brien County and the best shopping center in the county. By 1884, Sheldon became well known for its thriving businesses. Streets were not paved, and sidewalks were made with lumber.

The Sheldon Independent School District was organized in 1876, and a two-story school was built in 1879.

Throughout the years, many improvements marked the growth of Sheldon, with three railroads and two major highways passing through town, and an increasing population.

This is an aerial view of Sheldon in the 1940s looking northeast.

The early settlers set up places of business that would fill their needs, such as McKeever and Burkle Grocery, Lane's Bank, Bassett's Clothing Store, and lumber companies.

Sheldon had no paved streets until 1913, when Peter Trompeter and his son Frank put in a bid to pave 10 blocks and won the contract. They used concrete, sand, and paver bricks for those 10 blocks, which cost the city $33,450. The paver bricks were removed in 2018.

After World War II, automobiles became a problem in downtown Sheldon, so a traffic light was installed as a safety precaution.

Mayor Houlihan and Chief Jake Mulder developed a new rule in 1940 to speed up traffic on Saturday nights between 7:30 and 11:00 p.m. There would be no left turns allowed at the intersection of Ninth Street and Third Avenue. This would eliminate danger to pedestrians since a police officer would be stationed at that corner to direct traffic.

The American flag graced the center of the intersection of Ninth Street and Third Avenue for many years. It was removed in the early 1950s.

Several strings of Christmas lights were strung across the streets of Sheldon to enhance the season. Sheldon's first Christmas tree in 1872 was a four-by-four piece of lumber with sticks inserted to represent branches because they had no trees.

The oldest brick building in Sheldon was Hollander's 5-10-25 Cent Store, built in 1879. White's Hall was used for theatrical, social, cultural, and lodge activities on the second floor. Dr. Walter Cram's medical office was located upstairs, and a barbershop was in the rear of the building. In the 1950s, all the lawyers' offices were located on the second floor. Dr. Art Idema, a dentist, was also on the second floor.

The H.C. Lane building became the home of Wolff's Department Store, which was opened in 1916 by Theodore Wolff with the help of his wife, Sara, and family of Louis, Paul, and Sylvia. They operated the largest single department store in Northwest Iowa, but after 71 years in business, the store closed. Wolff's was known as the "outfitters of the entire family."

A lady was selected by a committee to reign as Soybean Day Queen during the Soybean Day celebration with the slogan of "Sheldon, the Uptown of Iowa." The chosen queen rode in the parade on Sheldon's float and in other parades in nearby towns.

Sheldon merchants placed items outside their stores on blocked off streets in the summertime just before the new fall and winter merchandise arrived in the stores. Reduced-priced bargains were realized by the shoppers, and the merchants could get rid of summer items and make room for fall and winter items. Hot dogs were served, and crazy costumes were worn by business leaders.

The parade was the highlight of the Soybean Days celebration, traveling through uptown Sheldon, residential areas, and by the park. Sheldon Soybean Days were held during the summer from 1959 through 1972, which was the last year for the celebration. Sheldon's centennial was in 1972. For several years, an annual celebration was held in June and was known as Prairie Queen Days. Commencing in 1972, the annual celebration was moved to Labor Day weekend and was renamed Celebration Days.

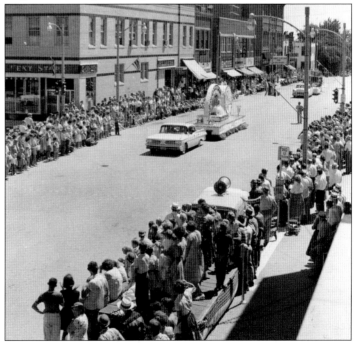

On special occasions, banners were strung across Sheldon's Ninth Street to attract the public's attention to important events. This banner promotes the Sheldon Commercial College in 1908. It was located in the Royce Hotel. Sheldon also had the Sheldon Normal College, which opened on September 4, 1893, to train teachers. It closed in 1900. Today, digital signs have replaced the banners.

Ten

RECOLLECTIONS AND NOTABLES

Sheldon was ideally situated for circuses to include the town in their schedules. It is strategically located between Sioux Falls, Sioux City, Des Moines, and Baraboo, Wisconsin. Three railroad lines passed through the town, which provided transportation for animals, tents, entertainers, and spectators. Both afternoon and evening sessions were filled to capacity. Circus personnel identified Sheldon as a town that loved to be entertained. It was a great thrill for the children to watch the circus personnel set up the big tent and performances of the animals and the entertainers in their lavish, sparkly costumes. Sheldon was a circus town from 1888 to 1915. Emmet Kelly, a world-famous Ringling Bros. and Barnum & Bailey clown, was a crowd favorite. George Hudson of Sheldon was a schoolmate of the Ringling brothers in Wisconsin. When the Ringling Bros. Circus came to Sheldon, Hudson and his family were given the best seats as guests at both performances.

At one of the early performances, a circus horse became sick and had to be taken to Dr. U.L. Shipley, a local veterinarian. The horse died and is buried at Hill's Park. A rumor circulated that an elephant died at the circus and is buried at Hill's Park, but that is just an urban legend. Another circus story that is true is that heavy rains fell on Sheldon when the circus was leaving town one year, and the circus wagons became stuck in the mud. The horses could not pull the wagons out, and elephants had to use their trunks to move the wagons. Ringling Bros. informed the city the circus would not return to Sheldon if the streets were not paved. The streets were paved in 1913, and the circus returned.

A yearly Sheldon District Fair was held at the grandstand with a racetrack on the west side of town. Entertainment included a midway, horse racing, bands, and entertainers in the grandstand. Jason Henry rode his well-known horse Miss Minta for 11 years. Henry's career as a sulky driver covered 48 years. He regularly drove at the Sheldon District Fair.

Regretfully, a different kind of event was held on June 21, 1924. A statewide Ku Klux Klan Konklave gathered on the west end of town with 25,000 members in attendance.

Sheldon has had a long history of service clubs; those currently active consist of Kiwanis (both Noon and Sunrise), Boy Scouts, Girl Scouts, and Fraternal Order of Eagles and Auxiliary. Two of Sheldon's oldest clubs are the Merry-Go-Round Club, established in 1903, and Chapter DU of the PEO Sisterhood, organized on November 12, 1908.

The Sheldon Historical Society and the Sheldon Prairie Museum hold induction ceremonies for hall of fame candidates. To qualify, the candidate must be nominated with a brief summary of qualifications, have been a resident of Sheldon during his or her lifetime, and have national recognition in the candidate's field or endeavor. A special room in the museum is dedicated to the hall of fame members for their contributions to their business, community, or profession.

George Hudson of Sheldon grew up in Baraboo, Wisconsin, and was a childhood friend of the five Ringling brothers. Hudson was influential in bringing the Ringling Bros. Circus to Sheldon for the first time in 1888, and the circus returned for six more engagements. This is a 1909 photograph.

The Ringling Bros. Circus needed 249 railroad cars to transport the circus to Sheldon and a 15-acre lot to set up the circus. Sheldon was a crossroads for three railroad lines that transported people from other cities and towns to attend the circus.

Normally the Ringling Bros. Circus did not set up in small towns because it wanted a large attendance, but Sheldon became a circus town. Ringling Bros. Circus had the largest circus attendance recorded, which was 26,000 people in Sheldon. Ringling Bros. merged with Barnum & Bailey and became "The Greatest Show on Earth" in 1918.

·SEASON 1915·

RINGLING BROS
WORLD'S GREATEST SHOWS

OFFICIAL ROUTE

ALLOW MAIL ENOUGH TIME TO REACH POINTS NAMED BEFORE DATE GIVEN.
GENERAL OFFICES NO. 221 INSTITUTE PLACE, CHICAGO, ILL.

DATE	TOWN	STATE	R.R.	MILES
August 9	Oklahoma City	Oklahoma	C. R. I. & P. Ry.	94
" 10	Tulsa	"	Frisco R. R.	118
" 11	Coffeyville	Kansas	A. T. & S. F. Ry.	117
" 12	Joplin	Missouri	M. K. & T. Ry.	84
" 13	Springfield	"	Frisco R. R.	95
" 14	Pittsburg	Kansas	"	125
	SUNDAY			
August 16	Topeka	Kansas	A. T. & S. F. Ry.	175
" 17	St. Joseph	Missouri	C. R. I. & P. Ry.	90
" 18	Creston	Iowa	C. B. & Q. R. R.	106
" 19	Chariton	"		59
" 20	Grinnell	"	C.B.&Q. and M. & St. L. R R's	93
" 21	Webster City	"	M. & St. L. Ry. and C. & N. W. R. R.	90
	SUNDAY			
August 23	Blue Earth	Minnesota	C. & N. W. Ry.	132
" 24	New Ulm	"	"	111
" 25	Spencer	Iowa	M. & S. L. R. R.	98
" 26	Sheldon	"	C. M. & St. P. Ry.	36
" 27	Algona	"	"	84
" 28	Austin	Minnesota	"	92
	SUNDAY			
August 30	Faribault	Minnesota	C. M. & St. P. Ry.	48
" 31	Red Wing	"	"	49
Sept. 1	Spring Valley	"	C. G. W. R. R.	77
" 2	Oelwein	Iowa	"	85
" 3	Postville	"	C. R. I. & P. Ry.	45
" 4	Anamosa	"	C. M. & St. P. Ry.	124

On the western edge of Sheldon, a racetrack and grandstand, which held 2,400 people, was where Jason Henry raced the Sherwood Farm horses that he trained and drove. Henry never raced his famous horse Lockhart in Sheldon, but he rode him back and forth in front of the Sheldon grandstand during district fairs.

Discover Thousands of Local History Books Featuring Millions of Vintage Images

Arcadia Publishing, the leading local history publisher in the United States, is committed to making history accessible and meaningful through publishing books that celebrate and preserve the heritage of America's people and places.

Find more books like this at
www.arcadiapublishing.com

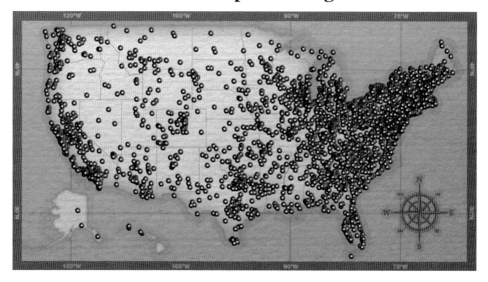

Search for your hometown history, your old stomping grounds, and even your favorite sports team.